THE PERSUASIVE BEAUTY OF IMPERFECTION

Poems by

Marguerite K. Flanders

Publisher Information

EBook Bakery
www.ebookbakery.com

Cover photo: Bill Azano
Author photo: David Flanders
Cover design: EBook Bakery

email: margieflanders@aol.com

ISBN 978-1-938517-32-7

Acknowledgments

Some poems in this collection first appeared in Poetry East, The Smoking Poet, and Poetalk.

Great thanks are due to two friends who were indispensable in the production of this book:

Michael Grossman, of EBook Bakery, who guided me every step of the way, with his encouragement and expertise, and Bill Azano, whose photo graces the cover, and whose gift of conversation helped me understand where I was going with this book.

I am grateful to all my poet friends, who keep me inspired, especially those in Ocean State Poets, the Origami Poems Project, and those I have met in various workshops, including my friends at the Narragansett and Warwick libraries, and the Medium Security prison in Cranston, RI. I also want to thank the following individuals who have shaped my work, through their teaching or just by example: Barbara Helfgott Hyett, the late Sarah Getty, Lisa Colt, Paul Hostovsky, Michael Mack, Lisa Starr, and my favorite poet, Carl Sandburg, who gave me the poetry bug to begin with.

I reserve my deepest thanks for the following people, who, each in their own way, made this book possible: My husband David, Carole Costanza, childhood friends Abbi Canney and Dee Brown, Richard Parker, Helen Lane, Jacqueline Sparks, my parents, John and Elizabeth Keil, and my brother, David.

For David

Contents

Personas and Stories

❖

Imperfect Beings

Matunuck, Rhode Island

Ocean heaves and washes herself
across the sand, folds her foam
into the tumble of waves.

Held and rocked by wind
rich with rose and wildflowers,
she wishes to go on and on.

But there is no life
without constraints.
Bound by her meager gifts,

she empties into what is vast,
the persuasive beauty and imperfection
of the shore's thrumming life,

and seamlessly joins
the narrative of sky
and earth in joyful accord.

After One More School Shooting

I fell out of love with the world,
and truth and beauty fell too.
I picked up the shards
of my soul, walked
out the door into the woods,
where the soil was too shallow
to bury anything. So I lay them gently
by the roots of a quivering sassafras,
turned and ran away.
Wind covered my brokenness with leaf
and bark, blessed it into oblivion,
and though I would never be the same,
some magic reduced my heartbreak
down to molecules too fine
to be perceived, too small to matter,
and reassembled them into a new
wholeness resembling hope.

And then, I fell in love again.

The Boy in the Boat in Watertown

2013, after the Marathon bombings

I'm there, or dreaming
I am, with a soundtrack
of bullets, screeching
violins, and my rapid heart
drum. Smothered by
stench of plastic air,
I am blooming blood,
deaf and drifting, a fugitive
who just lost a brother.

In the morning, I hear
your name on the tv,
over and over,
me warm in my home,
folding laundry
to get away from the blasts
of news. In the evening
I ply my violin
as if to save us all.

But when I sleep, I am
unforgiven, condemned
to my rancid boat,
putrid fear in my mouth,
twitching in pain at the explosion
of voices, surrounded and torn
to helplessness, nothing to be done,
just waiting.

A Small Quilt

Childhood was not roiling
thunder or holding out our hands
for an extra crumb. We didn't live
in a Dickens novel or under siege.
We had apple trees out back,
went to the beach in summer,
and I was pretty happy, though

disappointments and small fears
sometimes wore away at me.
Would Mommy ever die?
Would Daddy get another job?
Did we have to give away
Randy the dog, just because
he bit the mailman?

One day, on our front steps
I repeated the rhyme: *eenie meenie
miney mo, catch a nigger by the toe.*
Mommy stopped me, gently but
sternly, told me about bad words
and what they meant,
and I was ashamed.

Soon I learned that the world
hated black children, killed
people, was dangerous and dark
with war wounds and bombs,
poor children with no shoes,
while I had party dresses
and our home seemed safe.

So sometimes I just stayed
alone in my room,
cut out squares of cloth,
pink and black,
stitched them
together with my fidgety fingers,
a small quilt for the world.

As I Imagine It

JS Bach sits in a chair
cutting his toenails

doubting the last trill
of his last concerto.

Like a dictator crying
at his old dog's death

he feels the anguish
shoot through the glory.

I forget to feed the fire,
the woodstove dims.

At the piano, I try
to make Bach's notes

fly up like swallows
but I stumble on the sharps.

I have so many ways
to explore doubt,

while out the window
rain brushes daffodils.

I can almost smell their joy,
their lack of need

for any forgiveness

Longings

Where my mother lives, the walkers
and wheelchairs hang around
in the lobby, by the fireplace
with its impotent flames. The sad
stay alone in their rooms.

Some live for bingo, or exercise
class, reaching their arms slowly.
Others linger in the dining hall,
until the staff shoos them away.
My mother has learned to paint,
and goes on every field trip.

I think of my friend's horse, Mercy,
how warm her tongue was when
she sucked my fingers, and how later
she bolted from her corral, over
a stone wall, and down South Road,
her lovely lashed brown eyes looking
for a companion. And I wonder

if my mother will one day fly
across the edges of her enclosure,
looking for a friend, or a curved road,
forgetting who she is,
but not what she craves.

Lucky Strikes

My father lights the dark
to start the rose crinkle
of burn, drawing the world
with all its creations
into his accumulation
of language and sighs.

Then he breathes out
the dispersal, the blue
swirls rearranging chaos,
until everything means
and is in its place, unbound.
He hands me matches.

We resemble each other, we are
firekeepers, specters out back
on the porch, stubbing out our butts
in a cat food can full of water.
The hiss, sour rapture,
sacred ash of our mortal lives.

A Small Hope

The years have grown as thick as walls
around his heart. Youngness is gone,
long turned over into something else,

his sentence: the angry song going on
as if forever, and the lights too bright
and the smells of stress and fear

that penetrate the concrete,
like the sound of doors clanging
shut, the unguarded elements of loss

and restriction. But he does not
give in. He keeps something open,
finds the quiet he needs to survive.

With his hands in his pockets,
he breathes in the chill of the yard
and believes his exhale reaches the world.

His soul has softened into
a small flower he can see
in the dark. His will, his practice

keep him sane, he refuses to be
who they say he is, and when he dreams,
when he dreams, sometimes there is

a moment of hope, and he is back home.

What Is Random

Not you in your prison, nor me here in my studio's warmth,
reading your flightful words, images crackling with insight

as if I had just meant to write them myself, but then fell
into my own hidden pieces. So who are we, and where

do the fragrances in your memory meet up with mine?
If experience doesn't unite us, what about tree roots

mingling in summer's feast of soil, joined in their work
of weaving separate leaves, while the sun feeds us all?

The world tries to divide us up: age, status, name, crime.
The children we once were can now awaken,

yawning after dreams, reminding us that we did not
conjure these connections, they were always there.

Alchemy

Some walls are no more solid
than the boundary between
March and April, or the line
where wind and sky meet.
Divisions are mostly illusion,
to be puzzled out
like water/ice/steam
when lines blur.

Walking my road, I see
two men studying a stone goose.
One crouches, but he is not trying
to figure out the difference
between stone and life.

I think of Peter in his cell,
the razor wire rift in his marriage,
love neither fettered nor free,
and I want to practice dissolving
the difference between perfect
and imperfect. I want to learn
the art of one thing turning into
another, making distinctions
porous, meaningless
in the presence of all that is.

Soul Dyslexia

It's true, I see differently
I creep along slowly
on a crooked path
to enlightenment
I mix things up
and so I love balance,
palindromes make my day
1991 and 2002 were good years.
I read people backwards too,
think they like me when they don't
I'm always learning the hard way
but I know more than they think.
I split my infinitives,
trying so hard to not be
misunderstood
My brain parts entangle
when I play violin
and I long for fractal symmetry,
the unity of water
but I'm fine, really
and love is not beyond my ken
So you go be regular
and I'll juggle perception
and find a roundabout way
to truth.

Teaching Myself To Be

I start immune, trust
my tangle of functions, cocked
and happy, eager for the work.

I bask in the moon, wide as sky's mouth,
as if to fit earth, or sing
the medicinal, the actual.

And the sea, with its vibrato
of sleep, reminds me where
I am meant to be, strong with purpose,

pulling the water, its elemental burst
recalculating, smoothing my stress.
To tend my breath,

I play the violin, rest its treasury
against my cheek, unlearned music
begging to get out.

Firefly in the Sink

There's no reason for it to be there, no explanation
how it hitched a ride downstairs, below ground,

far from bushes or dark blue sky. It flashes green
on the slick white porcelain slopes, out of place,

foregoing the known for the unknown.
Like me, learning the violin, it plays

nervously into the tentative room. Unlike me,
it does not belong to a small civic orchestra,

it does not sit on a folding chair, too short
for its legs to get out of the way of its bow.

I cautiously lift its small strobing body
in a kleenex, through which its music sings

the silent flashes I long for from my violin.
I deliver it back out to the night, where I hope

it will find its way, which is what I hope,
always, for everyone, and for myself.

The Museum

In the museum of *I don't know*,
where my ignorances are on display
for all the world to see, rooms teem
with my deficiencies, rules I never learned,
the graces and subtleties never acquired,
whole corridors devoted to bits of science
and world history I somehow missed,
the Bach fugues I never played. There's
a storage closet for sports, how to score cricket,
and tennis, the love/deuce/game set match
mysteries my tennis-playing boyfriend
tried to teach me. It's me: I didn't want
to know. The museum is full of what
I was too stubborn to learn, thousands
of everyday facts I was too lazy to fathom,
gathering dust. So I rarely visit, and besides,
museums make me sleepy, make me head
for the back door, out to the spacious medicine
of stillness, where I gather up my own body
of knowledge, as useless to the world
as the rhythmic squeals of a swingset.
That much I know.

How To Find A Muse

I inoculate my heart with wisecracks, see the funny in what is torn. How else to engage a Muse, to bribe one, buy one, or buy two and compare? I row my boat backwards through the mud of years accruing like rivers of trash, just to get attention. In my scheming for inspiration I dance with brass door knobs, set off smoke alarms, infuse my words with sharp instruments, fleeting pain. If splinters and sunburn and broken glass punctuating my pressure points can get me a muse soon, then so be it. I invite all proposals that ignite chi, ban the drunks and vandals of inertia from crossing my threshold. And it seems I can hang in there, until the last acrid smoke clears, until I have snuffed out my old Muse, so I can welcome a new one, not so tired, not so restrained.

Summer Solstice

Sun has had its day, and still light remains.
I cut back the ferns and burdock. Rain has
instigated growth, soaked the finch feeder.
Night will come, resetting my heart's new clock.

Today I passed a curious white horse;
he hurried to the fence, threw his head back
and forth, showing off. I reached to feel breath
from his heaving nostrils, but I could not

touch him. He lost interest. It is sad
to miss connections, sadder to let go
if love stalls, when the weighted press of words
between friends becomes like a mute stone wall.

Be still as sun, I try to tell myself.
It burns but does not move out of its place.
How little I have learned, how unfinished
and expectant my soul still seems to be,

how lifted and then dropped from sky I am,
by the giving and take of gratitude.

Whirling

In the dervish of February,
roots mangle mild earth.
I walk the beach at dusk,
fidget with remorse
while my mother moves,
slow as a tree,
toward her death.

My arms ache for entrance,
the flickers of an urgent sea,
waves drawing the dark
like water from a well.

My lungs are restless, I miss
the white dog with his pleading,
the way he circled three times
before settling.

A surfer emerges
from the roiling,
sets down his board,
his back to the press of wind.
He kneels,
lays his forehead on sand.

Oh, how I long to be
that still.

Redemption

Taking off my coat of quiet,
I gently settle it on firm ground,
as if to still my trembling. Then I rest.

Mercy is not so hard to find,
if only I can put aside my trepidation,
threat of hard spring rain, even death.

But I am regretful and anxious,
turning my pockets inside out,
looking for treasures I think I lost.

I stand up, peer through the thickening woods,
then walk overgrown paths, following deer,
hoping they lead me to a clearing.

❖

Parting and Coming Together

Dear Universe

You let me in. Later you'll let me out.
Unlock and crack open my many
pods. Let seeds wheel and spin
in my catch of wind.
Shift me in grief's
grace, sing
in death's
voice
until
I know
your tune.
When rains
come to moisten
tangled roots, remind
me that each stroke of life
must cease, give up to what will
come next, each new imperfect beauty.

Where is the cat

When he looks down
he thinks he will fall
into a hole of shadows.

Suddenly he is old, hears
church music when his eyes
are shut, forgets he has eaten,

dreams of toilet paper and
watering cans, walks away
from his room into a hole

of shadows. The children
want to balance the checkbook,
talk to lawyers, he wants bread

and butter, wants to go home
to Tremont Avenue in the Bronx
to hear Violet sing, and his mother

praying to the God he has forgotten
he doesn't believe in anymore,
afraid of falling in a hole

of shadows, angry at the black women
who teach him to button his shirt and
watch him shower, all around

are people he doesn't know
and *Where is the cat, isn't she hungry?*
No Dad, that was at the old house.

Emptying

My father has not yet come
to an end, but he no longer
knows if his brothers are alive.
He has lost names and details,
like stones swallowed by high tide.
I can almost hear his mind
clicking like fingernails
under a cool white handkerchief.
He is trying and sorting and trying.

At the shore he faces the water,
swings his arms in circles to warm
his muscles. He talks constantly,
asks me again how old he is, as if
the question establishes our connection,
as if my answer, ninety one,
proves he is still on earth.

Sun snaps at our backs,
and he tells me a dream from last night:
he was holding a drawer full of his things,
carried and tipped them all into the ocean.

The breeze draws him forward, he turns,
 throws himself backwards into the water,
his scrawny frame sends up splashes
with each stroke.
Here he is absolved of all his fears.

I feel his emptying, though I know
there is more pain and release to come.
But the drawer has been spilled,
and he has already started to say goodbye.

Clarity/Nonsense

The hospital is full of groans,
sepsis, and pleading.

In these white corridors
doors open and close like mouths.

My father talks and talks all night.
He doesn't want to lie in bed

so they have strapped him to a chair,
his voice all urgency and abandon.

I inhale his face, I know
who he is, but now he speaks rhymes,

too many words tumbling in dumb
cruel magic, waiting to devour him.

He flutters, incantational, tells jibberjabber
to the room, sometimes makes sense.

He announces his death. His skull is full
of birthday candles, his tongue trills

in a rush of definitions, chanting equations.
He is the non sequitur, my mad hatter,

with his way of talktalktalk as I say
Goodbye.   He looks up,

Margie, when can I go home? he's waiting
for the room to spit out his bones.

And all I can say is
soon, soon.

At Hospice

My father is polite,
his rage spent.
I push his wheelchair
into his new room.

I have to urinate, he says
his carapace of dementia
split open for a moment.

So I lift his bony frame,
and he leans unsteadily
on me. We shuffle
to the bathroom,
with its yellow formica,
the striped bath mat.

What do I do? he asks.
I pull up his johnny, lift
his penis toward the toilet.
And when he is done,
I shake it, gently, as I have
seen my husband do.

In this new universe, we are
without shame, offering
each other the gift of tending
and being tended.

Exhausted, we walk
slowly to his new bed,
where he will set himself
to the labor
of his last breaths.

Initiation

While he was dying, I learned
the convoluted language of grief,
its secrets handshakes and signs.
Rainbows arched over the hospital,
I filled out forms, an ache in my throat.
Nurses taught me the mechanics,
the way *the body gives itself up*
like a rainbow dissolving. But my father
was not a rainbow.

The funeral director wanted his cause
of death, place of birth. I wanted to know
his pain, what kept him breathing so long.

Skies remained sullen after his eyes closed.
I worried about what we had not said,
undone by his ending. Death works
like a door: he was, now he isn't.
My voice slammed shut, and could not reopen,
even to say goodbye.

After My Father's Death

I swim nude
in the angry Atlantic,
stroking away from the sun.

Decline and light
struggle. Wisteria has slowed
its seeking. Acorns fall for the sake

of decay and creation. Fear.
Small hopes. The old terrier wants
the strong breath of a fan. Nothing to say.

I lie beside him, watch
the heavings of his grateful heart.

Going

she is near   stirs in her dream
            tired from the length of time
she has left behind
only the industry of breath remains
                with closed eyes she sees herself
clear as a voice   her fingers know
the earth she troweled burying
seed   a cool spaciousness
draws her   the halo of pain has lifted
                she is sudden   and parting
like waves   soon she will belong
everywhere   she unfolds
her last fright   sets her clock
to all directions   swirls
like luscious broth being ladled
                drops like a feather stone
that will never stop   if she can
only turn over   can only sing
          can only open that last window

Long Dark

Last night I forgot to sleep,
closed my notebook, traced
a labyrinth on the blotter,

spilled nothing, broke
nothing, did not cry for my mother,
though the knot of my navel

grows raw and red,
as if untying.

This morning I wear her rings
as if I am an heiress. I knock a vase
off the shelf as if I'm not.

Her death still
makes me unable to lie down,
and even the return of light

is a gift I'm too ashamed to receive.

Not That I Expect Anything To Be The Same

the summer of my mother's death,
when roses smell like old pages,
and clocks don't work,

but after she dies I dream I am swimming
and find a large stone floating,
as if gravity is a state we can choose or ignore.

In July wisteria blooms when it shouldn't,
my hair silvers up and vines grow
through the slats in the porch.
My truce with earth is overrun
with discord and bittersweet.
Air tastes like bad music.
Out the kitchen window
a green peacock is chased
by our cat, into the song of laurel.
Owls at night don't sound the same.

And I think back to when she was dying
when I hoped that laws of nature could be
disobeyed, when I could have asked her
to keep breathing, but instead I told her
she could let go,

and I wanted her to choose gravity,
but she floated away instead,
like a stone in a dream.

And summer thunders on, without her,
and I try to stick to what I know,
and tell myself, over and over,
despite the strange and blessed miracles,
and whatever they mean,
to just keep breathing, keep breathing.

Imperfect Ash

When the reasons for her suffering
seemed cruel, and obvious, when
there was no undoing the fall, when
it seemed she would not die, then did,

I thought of how she smiled, did not waste
complaint, a Buddha in her windowed room
of acceptance, calling my every gesture,
however inadequate, *perfect!*

After she died, fire transformed her done body,
and I wanted her remains to disappear and fly.
But because ovens are only so hot, and ash
is both fine and coarse, and not everything is perfect,

when I tossed the content of her life
it did not lift on wings, marrying the sky
and mating with cloud and spinning
around the earth ten million times.

Instead, bits fell in a small pile at my feet,
grey kernels of bone and tooth. Then I cried
for joy, and imperfection, grateful she had left
something behind for me to bend down and pick up,

this treasure to hold, this last gift, just for me.

As Above, So Below

The clouds of June,
soft and titanic,
gather over the shore.

Today, the word forever
demands my respect:
Sun's endless poem of fire.

The universe is rich with rock
and star. The microscope and
telescope scan the same vista.

I float between unlocked hands
of summer. What is there here
that needs to be held?

I miss my mother, who is
everywhere, her crooked toes
figuring out the sand.

Tone Poem
for Jean Sibelius

I succumb to the adjuvant moon.
The sea enters my pleasure.
When my mother dies, I inhale,
turn my back on trees and truth.

The declensions of grief close
doors, stutter my sight, until
I read that Sibelius saw a ribbon
of swans weave his sky.

For one day of this sad life,
I too see them. I fuss with pen
and paper, frantic to pin down
the gift. Then I wait.

Joy, I learn, is not a fluke.
It comes in its own time.
When I stay quiet, finally,
it sails me like white wings,

whatever the cost.

Night Vision

I tip my porch chair back
to scan the sky
for shooting stars.

I used to try to learn
the myths, trajectories
of constellations.

Now I want to see, not know.

I watched my parents die,
one, then the other.
I scrambled through
hospice brochures, books
by grief experts, wise Tibetans,
to figure out how it all works,
this dropping from life
one sense at a time.

Tonight I see what flares
and passes across
a secretive sky: not sun
or star, but pieces of fiery trash
tumbling into emptiness.

I watch what goes
and won't come back.

Voices Out of Context

When my parents came to visit,
Thanksgiving parched my throat.
He was tired of singing in the choir,
and talked too much. She pecked
at her words in the stumble of old age.
I hardly recognized them so far
from their home. I smoked out
on the porch in my long wool coat,
while they sat hunched inside, away
from owls and cold. Through
the window, I read their lips.
But they were speaking
their own language. My own silent keening
was for the inevitabilities, the big endings
to come. Far away, I heard a lost dog
being called, over and over. The flame
and dazzle was gone from the trees.
I knew someday I would hear voices
out of context, masquerading
as my parents talking to each other,
and in the machinery of grief,
even knowing it was not them,
I would hear each familiar word
falling like a last gold leaf
loosened from a split branch.

Remembrance

Rain plays the shingles like rhythm and blues;
the late May party next door moves inside.
Our dogs yawn, recolonizing the bed.

Grasses bend like sinners and crows gossip
until dark. Spiders repair their wet webs.
I wait for night's hands to clap thunder.

It is impossible to undo the spring, send it up
into the tipped and hidden bowl of moon.
I can't even sleep like the dogs,

tending only to the immediate.
Memento mori.
I turn away,
choose what endures, fold it into the now,

and the rest
down the drain like stormwater.

Moon

In the gold foam of sky,
above the tart stench of drought,
the clouds, clenched like dark hands,
cross the moon, then part
in a mudra of welcome.
Come back, says the moon,
Show us again how parting
can sometimes be a way
of coming together.

❖

Personas and Stories

The Storyteller
for Marc Joel Levitt

He's got an apple in his pocket,
his words interrupt the universe
whenever he chooses. Tonight

he wears a crumpled black hat,
tomorrow maybe not. He's down
on one knee, he's pretending

to pray and really praying. We lean
toward him, fall in and out of ourselves.
He's popping, he's a madman, he enters

us like a book he's been wanting to read,
he winks, he whistles through his teeth.
He hands the kids imaginary trees,

tosses the apple halfway to the sky,
as porous and spacious as a song.
And by the end, the world is real

and as bad and as good
as we imagined,
and we all know it.

That Moment

I stood by a highway
of swirling Utah snow
thumb out to the January night
alone   risking the fire
of my nineteen years

to find out.

Photo From 1969

That guy with the curly hair is Rick, he wants me
to run away with him, so we can burn up New York.
And there's Louie LaBelle, and Tommy and Sam, still

believing in Rick's play, his plan to start a troupe.
It's before everything falls apart; we've been up all night.
And there's me, barefoot, next to Rick, choosing to lose

the textbooks, the drone of dorms, to take up risk, trips,
writings and small spells, letters to drop in the river.
But look: clouds worthy of Moses loom, clasp

the horizon with their mean gold fingers, their prophesies
of dimming love as we pose by the Prudential Building.
Stacks of clouds thread the dawn into temporary clemency:

Even while Rick is thinking how to die, we all laugh.

Young and in Love

Before we met, we hitchhiked our lives,
secular and hopeful, throwing days like pennies
into water under bridges. We learned the cost
of sweetness, the gestures of trust imagined.
We gave ourselves away in the theater of change.

Then we met, oh how we met,
every whisper an incantation,
drawing down the heavens
into our heavy breathing and secrets.
My skies invited your rain. Your tuggings
encompassed me. Even the dry weeks apart
couldn't keep the seeds of love
from recapitulating ancient forms.
We warmed the kitchen of our bodies,
we were undiluted. We were married,
we were perfect. Climax was our religion.

Now, thirty years in, we've failed each other
a thousand times, and then fixed it, flushed with forgiveness.
We've been woven together beyond grief, joy and dogs.
We've survived the burnt pots, the floods.
We know the worst, and the sweet.

So for Valentine's Day, I give you a green scarf,
uneven rows into which I have knitted everything,
and left ellipses and elisions where unkissed kisses
and old grievances hide between stitches of us.
You sling its warmth around your neck,
and just like that, we're young again, and in love.

Lynnie Has Cut Her Long Hair Short

Lynnie has cut her hair, short
April is a story told two ways
What is lost wants to be found
in the awakening of roots and buds

April is a story told in twos
Chill wind through warm sun's song
The reaching, reaching of roots and tips
The slow/fast growing of many wings

Warm sun's promise through chill wind
Small eggs wait to be broken
The fast/slow month grows wings
Moon on her long hair, sheen of grief

What has been lost waits to be found
Lynnie has cut her hair, short

Out of Place

The empty bottle on the back step,
key on a crooked chain around her neck,
the rude fwack fwack of the screen door
as she flies out to the blacktop drive.

The one red sock on the clothes line,
the jagged cut of her hair, the uneven braids,
her black dress, the words she blurts out
that seem to come from somewhere else.

The goldfinch lying on the ground
under the window, with a broken neck.
In the mirror at night she sees a stranger,
dark disturbance of air and eyes.

Life cracks. She has lost her key,
her teacher says she is failing math.
She drowns, she wants to have something to say.
But the bottle is empty and the bird is done.

The Editor

Lydia is in bad humor, cuts her thumb
opening my envelope, frets that her daughter
will be refused by NYU. She doesn't like my font,
hates poems about mothers, she sees now
that her cat threw up on the oriental rug.

Her temples ache, my pages annoy her.
There's one line that gets her, though.
She too saw a sky open as a lily once,
when she was pregnant, and in love.
So she pours a cup of coffee, looks

out the window, takes up my poems again.
If I knew enough to hold my breath, I would.
But I am driving my mother to the doctor,
or playing violin, in the blush of a late
and petulant afternoon.

Lydia has never seen me cry or carry
logs to the woodstove, but she holds
my life in her hands, weighing my words.
When she throws away the envelope
that held my poems, she does not know

that I kissed it before sliding it
into the mouth of the mailbox.

Last Words

The poet takes his time,
lets his lines break
the silence gently,
no need for grandeur
when it is all just so true,
riveting in its accumulation
of insight, a good straight look
at everything he looks at.
And then there's this weaving,
this reticulation of meaning
that ties together his poems,
each to the other,

like a little wooden train
with wheels that turn
and an engineer in the front
who pulls a whistle,
over and over,
and you want the poet
to keep pulling the train
around and around
the hall of the library.
But finally, here comes
the caboose, the last poem,
which you hope will
go on forever,
and though you may not
remember every phrase
and line, because
of this ridiculous train
image that kicked in
halfway through,
and won't let go,

you're pretty sure
you'll keep, and hold,
and maybe even fondle,
the very last words
from his mouth.

The Woman Who Ate Her Own Words

She didn't do it just to show off; she felt she needed the nourishment of her own poems, required their grit and sweet, the fullness of their fiber. So she wrote a poem on a small square of thin rice paper, and as soon as ink dried, she began to nibble at the corners, chewed into the nouns and tired adverbs, punctuation and capital letters. It tasted chalky and sour, not what she expected, but she swallowed, worked through more lines and stanzas, gagging a bit, as it became harder and harder to want to make this work into food. The last words were excruciating to get down, dull and salty and nauseating in their sentiment, but she finally did. She closed her eyes, briefly, then it all curdled and curled up inside her, seemed to swell and unfold, words became tumors, meaning marinated by acid, paper and ink pressed on her esophagus like a fist. Then it all came back up, she could not help it. And when she looked at what lay on her desk, damp with bile, she watched a miracle: the fragments became immaculate, stitched themselves back together, and it was once again a whole poem.
Only this time, better.

First Day of School

Mama dragged me there, dark day.
I was begging for toys all the way down
the street, past bikes, and houses
hiding something terrible. My older brother
and friends were no help; they jumped
through puddles, laughed at the broken clouds
as we rounded the corner to the school
the color of dead wheat. My insides
were danger, a thresher, tossing and fluttering,
sick as a wet tea towel, sliced like raw meat.
I was hauled to the desert, through the shades
of hell. *Just think of it as visiting* Mama said,
but there was no return, all gone, I watched myself
break, daughter of a steel door. I wanted her
to carry me home on her back. But the world
and Mama lost interest, and I was a slave
delivered to the owners, all alone, choking
on my new deep endless sorrow.

Day At The Beach

A barbecued breeze moves
from the picnic area to the sea.
Sun scratches the shore with bright.

Down the beach, empty sand marks
where a row of cottages once stood,
not to be rebuilt, even the rubble gone.

A little girl, in a pink and green striped suit
holds a small stone up to her ear
like a phone, says "what? what?"

A poet enters the song of waves and surge,
not thinking of jellyfish or sharks. She strokes
against the tide, held close by water.

She wonders who would notice if she went limp
bobbing slightly just below the surface like flotsam.
Last week a man's heart's gave out; he died in water.

The wind picks up and waves flick her face
as she turns and turns, catching at breath.
Here is everything she loves and fears.

Massive clouds cross the sun like myth,
and people pack up to leave, colorful exodus
of towels, umbrellas, and trash.

The poet dismounts from the ocean
that has healed her since she was young.
And the little girl in the striped suit gets a call.

Dream

A tree fell on my car, and
I had to stay at my friend's.
We sat in his den on a blue day
bed with too many pillows. He held
my hand. I missed my violin,
trapped in the trunk; I wanted to cry.

He made me laugh, swept me
back on a cloud of chenille,
as if the dark menace of wind
that ransacked the night
was meant to be.

He rested his warm cheek
on my shoulder. In the morning
I washed my face with feathers;
we went for coffee at a deli on Rye.
Someone in a truck came,

hauled the confusion of branches
off my scraped and insulted car.
But I drove home content,
and we never spoke of it again.

My First Colonoscopy

Outside Spring opens up
like a fan, in revenge
for March's equilibrium.

I have fasted and purged
like a pilgrim; now I say goodbye
to my darkened grip on the room.

I am in a tree house
under my eyelids, telling
of my coming to terms

with whatever bursts into my life.
You'll ask how was my procedure.
I'll say I don't know; I wasn't there.

On The Dock

I'm standing on a dock with a lawyer, outside a restaurant,
where we've been talking and looking out the window
and watching what's left of the day's light fade, making
strategies for how to save all the trees in Rhode Island.
There are rows of yachts wrapped in white plastic, like
big pillows pulled up onto land. We walk by boats in the
water, soft light coming from within where people live.
Fred carries my laptop, says how light it is, and I say *hey,
you're carrying my life there, and if you drop it in the water
I'm done.* He's walking loosely before me, saying *no, I would
just buy you another one,* and I'm watching all my poems and
letters and other unbacked-up documents of the heart
swinging gently from his right hand.
It is not like me to be walking on a dock where people live,
or talking to a lawyer. Fred keeps going, and I follow,
to where the dock forms a tee, and there are white splotches
on the cross-dock, and we decide it is gull shit, and I wonder
why they only shit there, or why the marina only cleans the shit
off the walkway down to this place where the lights fade and
the black water laps pleasantly. It is both exotic and ordinary,
to be walking over water with a lawyer, who cares about
the future of our trees.
And for one moment I wonder what if I were here with
someone else, with whom the very conjunction of stars and
dark water could ignite something. What if I were much
younger, and Fred was not a lawyer. What if this was
not just a meeting about trees, but a beginning, a chapter
that almost didn't happen, but might have. And I look up,
and I look back, and I look down, and I think of the dangers
of the heart, the safety of fantasies and ambiguities and
distance and years, and I give it all up, like throwing
the laptop in the water, and I start to say to myself,
all will be revealed, but I realize much of it already is.

We walk back to my truck, and Fred's expensive car. He's still talking, and hands me my life in the black case, and I put it in the passenger seat. Now it is night, and I say goodbye to Fred, and by the time I put the truck in gear, I am completely back in my life, and off I go, passing the trees of Rhode Island. But all the way home, I can still see the way the dark water folded the glints and sparks into itself, the way we all bury some moments of light until we can deal with them, the way we find black cases to stash away our memories and stories and lovings, and then carry them down to the end of a dock, just to remind ourselves of how valuable and irreplaceable they are.

Veterans Cemetery, Ardennes
for my father

Empty handed
on the battlefield, they are
a river as it pours itself
through the reflection of moon.
They are many,
a silent bridge, walking,
passing off light
like flattery, stepping
over their own shadows
under eclipsed suns,
fluid and moving
and never coming back,
making space for new soldiers.

Me at One Hundred

Which I would be today, if I hadn't died seven years ago,
in a darkened hospice room, delivered of my stubborn
breath by the last loaded pink syringe of morphine,
after which the ugly nurse in the cat print scrubs yanked
the sheet back, pointed to my dark, blotchy calves,
saying *see, he will be gone soon.* And I wanted to rise up
in fury, punch her in the head. But no. After I was gone,
a parade of women dressed in black came; my daughter
called them *angels of death.* They stood around me, offered
their social work, funeral care, inappropriate prayers.
And this I found unseemly, and mildly embarrassing.
The family got through it somehow, the arrangements,
the service, getting rid of clothes, and in a way I am
one hundred, or at least that's the age of the small pile
of my ashes, all that's left of my spry, scrawny frame,
the hands that did magic tricks, played trumpet, the legs
that carried me to war and back, and oh my nimble feet,
with their way of never seeming to be still. Now I am still,
and to keep me close, my daughter will dump the charred
bits of me at the concrete corners of the foundation
of the studio being built in the woods, and there I shall
remain while she writes her poems, maybe listening
for my whistle, or the snapping of my fingers.
                    And I will try not to disappoint.

The Last Wave

When I am ready to put down my violin,
empty all my coffee cups and sock drawers,
hand over the keys, write myself
out of the poem, I will go down to the sea,
stand on a boulder, contemplate
my age and the mossy existence
I have accumulated around me.
On trembling cliffs and waves of memory,
the weight of what I know
will give way to what I do not know.
My deepest hungers will lap at an empty bowl,
my thirst gone. The bridge of years
will buckle under me, pleasant mist of distance
stretching in all directions, and even my hands
will seem comfortably new and unfamiliar.
And in this moment of quiet, while dusk
hangs on my shoulders like a queen's minky robe,
I will face the water, writing words up and down
my arms for the birds to read, patient
for the deep humming to claim me,
ready for the dissolving of tongue, eyes, self.
I will stand on a boulder for the last time,
without fear, ready to let go of earth and sea,
bring my joy to its logical conclusion,
decide upon the last wave rising up to meet me,
and ride it home.

Moment of Wind

February's fist knocks the back
of my throat, wind grabs breath,
my heart does two things at once:
pumppumping and alerting me
that my loves are many, full
of divinations pointing me
to my lineage, to who completes
me, who turns up in my dreams,
who and what I write, what
and who increases me. Wind
exhales, my blue hat tumbles,
I gather the wool between my fingers
before it touches earth, and
I think of my father raking leaves,
and then of my violin
with its half smile and voice
trying to be honey, but coming out
pine needles, and before
I can breathe again, the day goes bright,
a preview of enlightenment, a splash
of insight like cash spilling
on a sidewalk, like sails full
of combustion. What I mean is
that love, like breath and wind,
follows its own course and reason.
Its uncontainable rhythms
are meant to break free, turn us
over, catch and hold
our attention. Love stretches
us in all directions, offers us
all forms, we love all,
the way we love our mothers

and the wrens in the wreaths.
And my heart reminds me
that love won't take no
for an answer, I am a rose sucking
water up its stem, leaves at the tops
of trees licking sun, I have mastered
this merging, I am the eye
of my own storm, flickering
with mysteries and making room
for everything my heart requires.

About the Author

Marguerite Keil Flanders is one of the founding members of Ocean State Poets, a group that strives to bring poetry to all communities in Rhode Island, through readings, workshops and special events. She has led workshops for over 20 years, in libraries, schools, at conferences and Women's Centers. Her work has appeared in many publications, including *Boston Review, Yankee Magazine, Ballard Street Poetry Journal, Coal City Review, Comstock Review, Connecticut River Review, Caesura, Main Street Rag, Nimrod International Journal, Poetry East, Poetalk, Snail Mail Review*, and *The Smoking Poet*.

Since 2008 she has been part of a team that runs a poetry workshop every other Saturday, at the Men's Medium Security Prison in Cranston, RI. She has been interviewed, and featured in programs, about her work with prison poets. Margie is currently offering workshops and private sessions in her studio in Wakefield, RI. She can be reached at: margieflanders@aol.com

EBook Bakery

We at EBook Bakery know there are few things as pleasurable as encountering well-chosen words or an author's satisfaction when his or her talent is recognized. We also know the challenges writers face if they want their work published.

Until recently, the folks who determined if a book lived or died, publishing's "gatekeepers," chose manuscripts based on likely commercial success. That's understandable, but quality can become secondary, some worthy manuscripts get a thumbs down, and fine writers get discouraged.

This isn't new. You would be surprised by the list of authors whose works, considered classics now, were self-published after traditional publishers turned them down.

The EBook Bakery helps authors publish by benefiting from the digital revolution. Print-on-demand, EBooks and audiobooks permit inexpensive self-publishing so authors who believe in their work don't have to bet the proverbial "family farm" for it to come to market. There are technical considerations with self-publishing, but our digital know-how insures that a self-published book arrives as polished as one traditionally published.

The EBook Bakery guides authors through each step in the publishing process until the day when they first hold their paperback, EBook, or audiobook, and see it available through major retailers. From editing, interior book design, cover development, to setup and distribution, we work with fellow authors and improve their books. That's our passion and authors confirm it. See their comments and their books at www.ebookbakery.com

www.ingramcontent.com/pod-product-compliance
Lightning Source LLC
LaVergne TN
LVHW021620080426
835510LV00019B/2675